CW01020547

Take up Hockey

Principal contributor:
Norman Hughes
Great Britain and England men's national team coach;
Olympic bronze medallist 1984

SPRINGFIELD BOOKS LIMITED

Copyright © Springfield Books Limited and White Line Press
1990

ISBN 0 947655 80 8

First published 1990 by
Springfield Books Limited
Springfield House, Norman Road, Denby Dale, Huddersfield
HD8 8TH

Edited, designed and produced by
White Line Press
60 Bradford Road, Stanningley, Leeds LS28 6EF

Editors: Noel Whittall and Philip Gardner
Design: Krystyna Hewitt
Diagrams: Steve Beaumont and Barry Davies

Printed and bound in Great Britain

Photographic credits:
Cover photograph: Action Plus
Trevor Adams (Hockey Digest) 16, 23(t), 31
Graham Coltman (Hockey Digest) 19
Peter Luck (Hockey Digest) 11, 23(b), 28, 36, 38, 44, 49, 61
Supersport 6, 8, 14, 20, 24, 25, 26, 27, 29, 30, 33, 34, 39,
    40, 43, 45, 46, 47, 51, 56, 63

Contents

1

Introduction

Hockey is a fast and skilful game which is played in over eighty different countries. At any level it is a thrilling game which gives lots of fun to young and old, men and women. The age-groups start with mini-hockey for the under-twelves, and then there are colts (under 14), seniors (14–44), and veterans (over 45). Most hockey is played by single-sex teams, but some clubs also play mixed hockey. This wide range means that hockey can truly be a family sport.

Hockey can be modified to suit local conditions or different age groups, but throughout this book, unless stated otherwise, we describe the normal game of outdoor hockey, as played by men and women alike.

Wherever we have used "he", "him" or "his" in this book, it is intended to apply equally to players of either sex.

The aim of the game

The aim of hockey is very simple: your team of eleven players tries to move a hockey ball up the pitch and into the opposing goal by using hockey sticks alone. Meanwhile, eleven opponents do all they can to stop this happening, and indeed try to move the ball into the goal at your end of the pitch.

You may only hit the ball with one side of the stick, and only the goalkeepers are allowed to use hands or feet to control or move the ball.

> To play the game is good
>
> To win the game is better
>
> To love the game is best!

2
The players and the game

The players

A full hockey team consists of eleven players, one of whom is the captain.

Each team will contain a goalkeeper and a number of attacking players, midfield players and defensive players. However, in the very best teams, every player except the goalkeeper has to be good at both attacking and defending. Top teams work on the principle that when they have possession of the hockey ball they are all potential attackers, but if they lose possession of the ball then they all defend together.

Getting the ball or stopping attacks is not just a matter of luck: you must learn to position yourself effectively on the field. Successful players are effective at "marking" opponents by staying close to them so that they do not have the freedom to attack.

The positions

Sweeper/fullback

These players need to be good ball winners and to have the ability to pass hard and accurately over long distances. They need nimble footwork, and should be able to spot the main danger area of an opponent's attack.

Right half or right back

These players need good speed and mobility. The right half often starts counter-attacks; by supporting the forwards effectively, he can make all the difference in a very close-fought game.

The right half or right back normally marks the opposing left-wing player.

Centre half or centre midfield

The main job of the centre half is to collect passes from the defence and then feed them accurately to the forwards. He should play up and down an imaginary central channel of the pitch so that he can quickly and easily transfer the ball across it. His presence in the centre can also keep the opponents' attacks to one side of the pitch. You will sometimes hear the centre half referred to as "the engine room of the team".

Centre back

The centre back marks the opposing centre forward tightly, so he must be fit enough to stick close to his opponent and be a good tackler. Centre backs are normally strong physically, so that they can cope with the knocks sometimes generated when marking tightly.

Left half or left back

The left half's main job is to mark the opposing right-wing player. Right wingers are usually very fast sprinters, so it is important that the left half has good speed. Tight marking and strong tackling are the main defensive abilities of the left half; having won the ball, he must also be able to transfer it across the pitch accurately, and so must develop a precise hit pass.

Inside forwards

The inside players in the forward line are the inside right/right-midfield and the inside left/left-midfield. These are the players who usually set up successful attacks by threading intelligent passes through the defence. They need good close ball control, wide vision and the ability to think quickly to spot the best pass to give, speed, stamina and goalscoring instincts.

Wingers

The right-wing/right-attack and left-wing/left-attack players need pace and good close ball control. They need to be able to spot the space to use behind the defenders. Top wingers have goalscoring instincts and can hit hard accurate crosses (cross-field shots). It is particularly important for left-wingers to develop the ability to hit the ball effectively even when their weight is over the right leg. This is called "hitting the ball off the wrong foot".

Centre forward

Centre forwards need pace, strength and good close ball control to enable them to find space and get to the ball first in a crowded penalty area. Goalscoring instincts are vital, together with the ability to anticipate crossed passes.

Goalkeeper

Confidence, bravery, agility and quick reflexes are all needed by the goalkeeper. Good concentration and the ability to spot the angle of the shot quickly are essential.

Team formations

Just as in soccer and other field games, the teams may use different formations on the field. Figure 1 shows two teams lined up for the start of a match. The top team is using the "5-3-2-1" formation, while their opponents use "3-3-3-1-1".

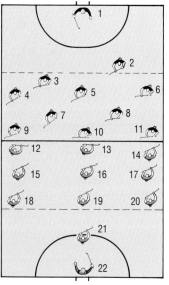

Figure 1 Two typical team formations

KEY
1 goalkeeper
2 left full back
3 right full back
4 right half
5 centre half
6 left half
7 inside right
8 inside left
9 right wing
10 centre forward
11 left wing
12 left striker
13 centre striker
14 right striker
15 left midfield
16 centre midfield
17 right midfield
18 left back
19 centre back
20 right back
21 sweeper
22 goalkeeper

10

The strength of the 5-3-2-1 system is that the triangles it forms give good support to the player on the ball and good cover against attacks. The 3-3-3-1-1 system leaves one player — the sweeper — behind the defence ready to spot danger and sweep up any attacks or long through balls.

In the modern game it is common for all the players to go forward in attack and to run back into defence when necessary. This sometimes makes it difficult to distinguish between the positions during play.

The officials

On the field, two umpires enforce the rules of the game and ensure that it lasts for the correct length of time. Unlike a soccer referee, who is on the field at all times, hockey umpires follow the play from the sidelines, only venturing onto the field when necessary. It is a tradition of hockey that players should not question the decision of an umpire. Everyone makes mistakes, both players and umpires, but hockey encourages everyone to get on and concentrate on the game and on having fun.

Good umpires keep play flowing fast and fairly.

Duration of play

A full game of hockey consists of two 35-minute playing periods, separated by a five-minute interval. The
teams change halves after the interval.

The pitch

The hockey pitch, or field of play, is laid out as shown
in Figure 2.

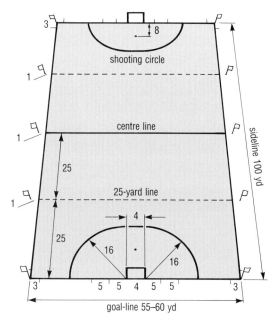

Figure 2 The hockey pitch; all dimensions shown are
in yards, as defined in the rules.

3

Equipment and clothing

Before you spend money on your own equipment, you should get the feel of the game by trying it out. Many schools and clubs have stock equipment for beginners to use.

The stick

Whether borrowing or buying, take particular care when choosing your stick, because choosing one of the wrong length or weight can prevent you from developing the correct skills.

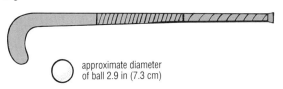

approximate diameter
of ball 2.9 in (7.3 cm)

Figure 3 The hockey stick: its maximum weight is 28 oz (794 g) and the minimum weight is 12 oz (340 g).

The stick must be able to pass through a 2 in (5.1 cm) ring. The head of the stick must be made of wood, and it must not have any sharp edges.

The left-hand face of the stick is flat: this is the playing face, and you must always strike the ball with this side, regardless of whether you are naturally left-handed or right-handed.

Most adult players use a stick which is about 36 in (92 cm) long, weighing approximately 20 oz (570 g).

If your stick is too long you will find it impossible to hit the ball properly, because the distance between it and your feet will be too great. This makes it difficult to control your swing and can lead to dangerous shots. Play will also be uncomfortable, because the top of the handle will feel awkward against your stomach.

With a stick of the correct length, the swing will feel comfortable, and you will easily be able to align the stick face with the ball to hit or push it. This action is called "addressing" the ball.

As a guide, you will find that a stick will be about the right length if the top of the handle reaches your hips when the head is on the ground beside your feet.

The ball

Match hockey balls weigh between 5½ oz (156 g) and 5¾ oz (163 g). The rules allow various types of hard materials to be used. It is usual for young players to use a lighter ball (4 oz; 113 g), and you should bear this in mind if you are buying a ball to use for informal practice.

Clothing

Look good, feel good, play well! Take a pride in your appearance and you will soon begin to feel like a top player. You will need a shirt which fits comfortably and does not get in the way as you swing your stick. Skirt or shorts, and football-style socks, complete the playing outfit.

A tracksuit is worthwhile, so that you stay warm before and after games, and also during coaching sessions.

Footwear

Although more and more hockey is being played on synthetic pitches, grass is still much more common.

Flat-out play on synthetic surfaces is tough on feet and ankles.

Your footwear must suit the surface:

- For grass, you will need a pair of good quality soccer boots.
- For synthetic pitches such as Astroturf, you will need training shoes with ridged or pimpled soles.

Choose your boots or shoes carefully. Hockey is a game of stop, start, change direction, turn and sprint, so your feet and ankles need firm support and protection. Get the best footwear you can afford.

Protective equipment

Shinguards

To prevent injury from the ball or from other players' sticks, shinguards are essential on the hockey field. Special hockey shinguards made from lightweight plastic or foam will effectively protect both shins and ankles, but many players start by using soccer or rugby shinguards. If in doubt, get advice from an experienced player or at any good sports shop.

Gumshield

When you are young it is easy to believe that no accident will happen to you during play, and hard to realise just how precious your teeth are. However, although hockey is a safe sport, accidents can happen, just as in many other sports, so it is better to be safe than sorry. Therefore I strongly recommend the use of a gumshield right from the start. If you have this made for you by your dentist, it will be comfortable, and you will soon get quite used to it.

Goalkeeping equipment

Although the clothes used by the field players are simple and not very expensive, the goalkeepers need special protective equipment which is in a different class. The goalkeepers are the only players permitted to use body-protectors, pads, kickers, gloves, elbow pads, helmets and face masks.

Because of its specialised nature, most of this is often provided by the school or club. A hockey ball can be hit very hard at goal, so goalies should never skimp on equipment: fear of injury would prevent you from making bold saves; actual injury might well put you off the game for ever.

Take trouble in selecting this equipment so that you are comfortable and well protected, yet can move as fast and freely as possible.

A full set of protective equipment is essential if a goalkeeper is to play confidently and safely.

Helmet
A proper hockey helmet and face mask is essential. Try a few different masks if you can, and select the one which allows you the best all-round vision.

Gloves
Goalkeeping gloves should be well padded. This is particularly important on the left palm to ensure that you don't feel pain when stopping a fast shot. Both gloves need enough padding to protect your knuckles, but you must be sure that the right one is flexible enough to allow you to keep a good grip on the stick at all times.

Leg-guards
Special goalkeeping pads protect your legs without being unduly heavy. The modern style uses cane bars to stop the ball. Although you will be well aware that the ball has hit your leg when you are wearing pads, you will not be hurt by it.

The size of pads is limited by the rules: each may be no wider than 12 in (30 cm) when on the goalie's leg.

Although they are sometimes used, cricket pads are not really suitable because they fit too closely around the leg. In hockey you need as much flat surface as possible to stop the ball.

Kickers

Kickers give additional protection to the feet and ankles. The new foam-wedge kickers are light, comfortable and give good protection. They allow you to develop an effective style of clearing the ball from the goal by kicking it like a football.

Body protection

All goalies need protection for the chest and abdomen, and plastic body armour of the type originally developed in ice hockey is often used. Female players often wear a combined protection plate, but male players need a chest protector and a separate "box" or abdominal protector, which is absolutely vital.

Goalkeeper's stick

Most goalkeepers use a light stick, often of the type used in indoor hockey, because it is easy to move quickly and light to carry. For most of the game, the stick is held with the right hand only.

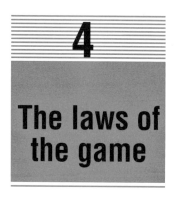

4

The laws of the game

In many ways hockey is similar to soccer. Each team has eleven players and tries to score by getting the ball into the opponents' goal. Patterns of team play, marking, running off the ball and support play are all very similar to soccer, but there are also important differences. The following list of rules is not complete, but it will allow you to understand the main elements of the game so that you can play it fairly. A complete set of official rules can be obtained at low cost from your national governing body (see page 64).

The rules of hockey are designed to allow fast and skilful play while reducing danger to a minimum. Good players play hard, but place skill and fair play above all.

Starting the game

The toss-up
Immediately before play starts, the captains toss a coin. The winner has the right to choose either the direction to play or to make the opening pass-back.

Pass-back
At the beginning of each half of the game, and after each goal, play starts with a *pass-back* from the centre of the pitch. As the name suggests, the ball is passed in such a way that it does not go over the centre line until it has been touched by another player. Until the pass-back is made, the opponents all have to be at least 5 yards (4.55 m) from the ball. With the single exception of the player making the pass-back, all others have to be within their own halves.

Once the player taking the pass-back has hit the ball, he may not attempt to play it again until it has been touched by another player.

The first pass-back is taken by a member of the team which did not have the choice of ends. After the interval, the other team takes the pass-back, and after each goal it is made by the unsuccessful defenders.

Scoring

The only way of scoring in hockey is to play the ball fairly into the opposing goal.

A goal is scored when the ball passes completely over the goal-line between the posts and under the cross-bar, having been hit (or deflected by an attacker's stick) from within the shooting circle. The attacker who hits the ball can be outside the shooting circle, provided that the ball is within it at the time of the shot. The goal is still scored if the ball touches one or more defenders before entering the goal.

If the ball is hit by an attacker from outside the circle and then deflected into the goal by a defender who is anywhere inside his 25-yard (22.90 m) line, no goal is scored. Play then resumes with a long corner.

Even if it gets past the goalie, a shot will only count as a goal if the ball is within the shooting circle when the attacker hits it.

During play

Backsticks
Only the flat front face of the stick may be used for controlling or passing the ball. If you use the back, the umpire will stop play and award a *free hit* (see page 24) to your opponents.

Feet and hands
The ball cannot be kicked or stopped with your foot, hand or leg unless you are the goalkeeper. You must always use your stick; if you should drop it or break it, you may not take any part in the play as long as you do not have the stick in your hand. The penalty is a free hit for your opponents. However, you will not be penalised for protecting yourself with your hand against a high ball which you could not otherwise avoid.

Dangerous play with the stick

Dangerous play with the stick is known as "sticks". You are not allowed to raise your stick in a dangerous manner. If you swing it wildly in a crowded area, the whistle will be blown for dangerous play and the umpire will give a free hit to your opponents.

The umpire will also blow for "sticks" if a defender saves a probable goal by raising his stick above his shoulder. A penalty stroke is awarded to the attacking side.

Dangerous play with the ball

You commit a foul if you lift the ball through or into a group of players, because this is considered to be dangerous play. A free hit to the opposition would result, unless the offence is committed within the shooting circle, in which case a penalty corner is given.

Obstruction

You are not allowed to shield the ball with your body or stick to prevent your opponents from playing it. If you do this, you will be penalised for *obstruction*. Always bear this rule in mind, as obstruction is not always easy to avoid. For example, if you are facing your own goal you must try not to position your body between the ball and an opponent who is close enough to tackle you. The obstruction rule is a difficult one to understand at first, but it is essential to prevent rough and dangerous play. If you obstruct, the umpire will award a free hit to your opponents (see page 24).

A very illegal stick tackle by the player on the left during a USSR v Holland match

Tackling

You are not allowed to hit an opponent's stick, hold it or interfere with it. You must play the ball cleanly. Similarly, you must not shove, kick, trip or strike the body of your opponent. A free hit (or penalty corner) results if you commit such an offence.

Offside

You will be in an offside position if you are in your opponents' 25-yard (22.90 m) area and nearer to the goal-line than the ball, *unless* there are two opponents nearer to the goal-line than you are. One of these can be the goalkeeper.

Although you may be in an offside position, you will not be penalised for that alone unless you attempt to play the ball, obstruct or distract an opponent, or otherwise take advantage of your position.

If you are in an offside position, you will become truly offside at the moment one of your team-mates passes the ball to you — *not* at the moment you receive it. However, if you run forward onto a pass from another member of your team, provided that you were not offside when the ball was passed, you will not become offside during the passage of the ball.

If the umpire declares you to be offside, a *free hit* is awarded to your opponents. This is taken from the point where the offside occurred, unless you were less than 16 yards (14.63 m) from your opponents' goal-line; in that case the free hit is taken from the point 16 yards (14.63 m) from the goal-line which is in line with your offside position.

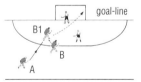

Figure 4 An offside example: A has the ball and plays it to B1; B runs forward to take the ball at B1, and scores. Will the goal be allowed?

A is not offside, because there are two defenders between him and the goal-line. B is not offside either, because there were two defenders between him and the goal-line *at the moment* when A passed the ball forward. The goal will be allowed!

Re-starting play when the ball is off the field

The ball can go out of play for a variety of reasons, and there are several different ways of getting the game going again.

> **In or out?**
> In hockey, the ball remains in play until it has passed completely over the boundary line. If it touches the line, it is still in play.
>
>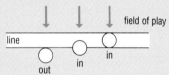
>
> **Figure 5** The ball must be *completely* over the line before it is out.

Hit-in

If the ball is played over the sideline by a member of one side, play is restarted by a member of the other side pushing or hitting the ball in from the point at which it left the pitch. No opposing player may be nearer to the ball than 5 yards (4.55 m). The ball must be stationary when hit and must not be raised in a dangerous manner.

16-yard hit

If the ball goes out of play over the goal-line off the stick of an *attacker* (for example, if an attacker shoots wide or loses control and runs the ball off the end of the pitch), one of the defenders restarts the game from a spot on the pitch exactly opposite where the ball crossed the goal-line, and not more than 16 yards (14.63 m) from that line.

Long corners

If the ball is played unintentionally over the goal-line by a *defender*, the attacking team takes a hit or a push from a spot on the goal-line within 5 yards (4.55 m) of whichever corner flag is nearer the point where the ball crossed. This is known as a long corner.

Re-starting play after stoppages and fouls

Penalty corners (short corners)

Penalty corners are one of the special features of hockey. They are awarded against the defending team for deliberate offences within the 25-yard (22.90 m) area or for accidental fouls within the scoring circle.

The game is also re-started with a penalty corner if a defender intentionally plays the ball over the defence goal-line to stop an attack.

A penalty corner is taken by an attacker hitting or pushing the ball from a spot on the goal-line 10 yards

(9.14 m) or more from the nearer goalpost. This spot may be on either side of the goal. The attackers can choose which side to play from. All the attacking players must stand outside the circle; five of the defending team stand behind the goal-line until the ball is put into play. The other six defenders must retire over the halfway line. All the players on the pitch must remain in position until the ball is played. To score from a penalty corner, the ball must be stopped by a second attacker and played into the goal. There is no score if it simply bounces into the goal after being deflected by a defender.

Some care must be taken with the first hit at goal which follows a penalty corner: as it enters the goal, the ball has to be below the top of the 18-inch-high (46 cm) boards at the base of the net.

The short corner offers a good opportunity to a well-practised team, and many goals are scored from them.

*For a penalty corner, attackers (**above**) line up just outside the shooting circle.*

*Five of the defenders must stand behind the goal-line. Here (**right**) all five players are packed into the goalmouth. As soon as the ball is hit, some of them will run out to play their part in the defence.*

Penalty strokes

A penalty stroke is awarded for a deliberate foul within the circle or for an accidental offence which apparently prevents a certain goal.

Like the penalty kick in soccer, it becomes a contest between one attacker shooting from the penalty spot and one defender — usually the goalkeeper — who has to remain stationary on the goal-line until the ball is struck. The spot is 7 yards (6.40 m) in front of the goal, and the ball may be pushed, flicked or scooped at the goal. The attacker can take one pace towards the ball to make the stroke, and there is no limit on the height at which the ball can enter the goal.

The ball can enter the goal at any height from a penalty stroke.

Free hits

The penalty for a breach of the rules in most areas of the pitch is a free hit to the non-offending team. Umpires also have wide discretion to penalise rough, dangerous or unsporting play, and will usually do this by awarding a free hit.

A free hit is normally taken from the point where the offence occurred. The following points must be observed:

● The ball must be stationary when it is hit.

● No player from the opposing team may be within 5 yards (4.55 m) of the ball.

● The hit should be along the ground: the ball must not be lifted intentionally.

● The striker may not hit the ball twice: once the free hit has been taken, he must not play the ball again, or even approach within playing distance of it, until another player from either team has touched it.

Taking a free hit

Bully

The bully is the way the game is re-started after injury to a player or if both sides commit simultaneous fouls.

To bully, the ball is placed on the ground at the point where the game is to re-start. One player from each team takes up a position which would allow him to strike the ball squarely in the direction of the opposing goal-line. Immediately the umpire blows his whistle the players tap their sticks on the ground just behind the ball and then against each other above the ball. This is repeated twice more without stopping before the players compete to hit the ball, which puts it back into play.

During the bully, all the other players have to remain at least 5 yards (4.55 m) from the ball until it is put into play.

Advantage

In the interest of keeping the game flowing, umpires will not normally stop play for technical offences which do not give any advantage to the offending team. This is called "playing the advantage rule".

5

Basic skills

You can practise these basic skills of hockey on any flat surface if you have your own stick and a ball. Many good players have built up their game from scratch by starting on a tarmac drive or patch of grass.

Grip

Hockey is a right-handed game, and regardless of whether you are normally right-handed or left-handed, you should use the same basic grip:

● The left hand should be at the top of the stick, and quite firm

● The right hand is a comfortable distance (8–12 in; 20–30 cm) lower down the handle, with the grip more relaxed than that of the left hand.

The distance between the hands is adjusted depending on the distance of the ball from the body and the skill being performed (such as a hit or a push).

When you have mastered the basic grip, experiment and improvise with minor adjustments to see which grip suits which skill best.

The basic grip: Moira McLeod of Scotland in action during an international match. Note how the grip with her right hand is still quite relaxed so that she can make adjustments until the moment she strikes the ball.

The correct grip is essential in developing the skills you will need to play effectively, and left-handed players have to concentrate really hard early on to get used to it. If you are one of these, do persevere — some of the best players in the world are left-handers. This is because they are normally stronger than right-handers when a one-handed tackle or a left-side tackle is needed.

Running with the ball

Running while keeping the ball under control — *dribbling* — is a vital skill of the game. If you can do this, you can move the play into open areas of the pitch, away from your opponents. This is known as "creating space", and it can often lead to goal-scoring opportunities. When you dribble the ball in hockey, your body will need to be slightly crouched while running. This can be uncomfortable at first, but frequent practice will gradually strengthen your back and leg muscles.

Running with the ball and keeping it under control while you are under pressure is an advanced skill of the game.

There are different ways of dribbling:

The forehand dribble
In the forehand or *open-side dribble*, you keep the ball to the right of your body as you run. The main points to concentrate on are:

● Use the normal grip.

● Keep your stick head close behind the ball.

● Keep the ball ahead of your body and just outside your right foot, so that your running action is not restricted.

Close control during a forehand dribble

● Try to avoid letting the ball get too close to your feet. You need to be able to see well ahead in case there is the opportunity to shoot at goal or to split the defence with an accurate pass.

Turning the stick

Forehand dribbling would be much easier if you could occasionally use the back of the stick to check the ball or bring it under control, but the rules prevent you from doing this. The answer to this problem is to learn the trick of rapidly turning the stick in your hands, so that you can use it toe-downwards to contact the far side of the ball whenever you need to. Here's the way to do it:

● Hold the stick horizontally in your left hand only, with the toe pointing upwards.

● Turn it to the left (anti-clockwise) as if you are turning a door knob, until the toe points downwards.

● Adjust your grip until you can turn the toe of the stick from vertically upwards to vertically downwards. Get used to the feel of this position.

● Grip the shaft of the stick normally again with your right hand.

● Once you have the feel of the position of your left hand and the knack of turning it, you will be able to relax your right hand so that the stick can roll easily as needed, gripping it firmly again only when the toe is pointing straight up or straight down.

The stop dribble

The stop dribble is a reverse-side dribble, and so relies on the technique of turning the stick. As the name suggests, you use it to slow the ball and stop it running away from you. It is also a very effective way of changing direction during the dribble. The main points to concentrate on are:

● Turn the stick over the top of the ball by twisting your left wrist in an anti-clockwise direction.

● Let the stick rotate in your right hand.

● Concentrate on keeping the stick head as close to the ball as possible: if you can, keep it in contact.

● Dribble the ball just in front and to the right of your body, so that you can run smoothly.

The stop dribble will allow you to develop a change of pace when running with the ball; this can help to get you through your opponents' defences. Start practising this skill by walking with the ball and then stopping it; progress to jogging, and finally to running quickly.

A light grip with the right hand allows the stick to be turned fast with the left one.

The Indian dribble

This is a more advanced development of the stop dribble. The ball is swept across in front of you in both directions to try to wrongfoot an opponent.

Start practising this skill while standing still, and gradually build up speed until you can do it at a fast run without losing control of the ball. Top players can change sides 90 times a minute!

Start with the ball in front of your right foot and your weight supported mainly by your right leg. Drag the ball across to your left foot, and at the same time transfer your weight to your left leg. Stop the ball by turning the stick over with your left hand. The key points are:

- You should use a wide grip, hands apart, as for running with the ball

- Your feet should be about shoulder-width apart

- Your knees and body should be slightly bent

- The ball should be a comfortable distance from your feet (18 in–2 ft; 45–60 cm).

When you can run and switch the ball from side to side, you must try to vary the distance between changes of direction; the more variety you can introduce, the more you will be able to confuse your opponents.

Dribbling at speed with the stick reversed. Note how a wide grip is kept on the stick, and the ball remains between 18 in and 2 ft (45–60 cm) from you. Both knees and body should be slightly bent.

6

Passing skills

Hockey is a team game in which success often depends on your skill at passing the ball accurately and sometimes powerfully to your team-mates. You can use several different shots to make a pass, and you must learn to pass the ball in any direction. It is also very useful to learn how to disguise where you intend the pass to go.

The forehand push

Grip

Use your normal grip on the stick, and position yourself sideways-on to the ball, with your left shoulder pointing in the direction of the pass.

Position

Your feet should be just a little more than shoulder-width apart, and your knees slightly bent. The ball should be a comfortable distance from your body and slightly nearer to your left foot than to your right one. Lean slightly to the right, so that your weight is supported by your right leg.

A forehand push being used for a shot at goal from a penalty corner

Making the stroke

- Imagine that your stick is an extension of your right arm, and push the ball with the head of the stick as you transfer your weight to your left leg.

- Straighten your right leg as you make the stroke; your head should be further forward than your left toe as you send the ball on its way. You should feel as if you were pushing "through" the ball, controlling the stick mainly with your right hand.

- Follow through with your stick in the intended direction of the pass. This follow-through is very important.

You can add power to this push stroke by speeding up the weight transfer from right to left leg and by making your right hand overtake your left one during the push.

When you have gained confidence and experience, you will not need to look down at the ball all the time: you will be able to look around to locate your other team members. Try passing the ball while looking directly at the eyes of your team-mate. When you can do this quite naturally, you can disguise your intended pass by looking in a different direction.

The slap push

The slap push can put more power into a pass. The grip and technique are basically the same as for the push; the stick head remains in contact with the ground, but starts from further behind the ball.

"Open" and "closed"

The expressions *open* and *closed* have a special meaning when applied to the face of your stick during a stroke.

If the toe of the stick is slightly behind the shaft as the ball is addressed, the stick is said to be open. If the toe is slightly ahead, the stick is closed.

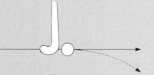

Figure 6 An open stick sends the ball slightly to the right of the direction of stroke.

When the stick is used on the right of your body, the expression "hitting on the open side" is sometimes used; the opposite of this is "hitting on the reverse".

Lisette Lejeune of Holland makes a fine slap push with a full follow through.

The forehand hit

While you will use the push pass very often, the more powerful *hit* is the way to pass the ball over longer distances and to shoot at goal.

Grip and position

Your left hand remains in position at the top of the handle, and you slide your right hand up close to it.

Your body position should be similar to that for the push, with the left shoulder pointing in the direction the ball is to go. Keep your feet comfortably apart, your knees slightly bent and the ball almost in line with your left toe.

Technique

Keeping your eyes on the ball, swing your stick back, letting your wrists relax to "open up" the face of the stick (see panel).

Your weight should now be on your right foot; as you swing the stick down in an arc through the ball, transfer your weight to your left foot.

Points to watch

● Tighten your grip on the stick just before it hits the ball.

● The arc of the stroke should follow through along the line of the pass or shot.

● Keep your head down and your eyes on the ball until the stroke is completed.

● Try to accelerate the head of the stick on the down-swing by pushing through with your right hand.

Variations

The forward hit described above is quite easy to master, but you will need to develop variations too: sideways hits are useful.

The usual way of hitting the ball to the left is to strike it when it is ahead of your left foot and with your left foot forward. However, you can also experiment with hitting it off your right foot, as this adds an element of disguise, and can surprise your opponents — including their goalkeeper.

Hitting to the left, off the right foot. Note the close grip, and see how the player's eyes are focused completely on the ball.

Hitting the ball from left to right is much more difficult: unless you reverse your stick, you have to move yourself around the ball so that you can approach it from your normal hitting position. An alternative answer is to use the reverse-stick hit described on page 35.

As you become more confident with your hitting practice, you can learn to disguise the direction of your pass by opening or closing the face of the stick with a last-minute flick of your wrists.

Reverse-stick push

This is the most effective and easily controlled of the reverse strokes. It is used for passing the ball over short distances when you have not got time to get your feet and body round for the forehand push.

The ball is pushed in a similar manner to the normal push but in the reverse-stick position. The ball should be near the front foot so that the stick will be at at an angle of 45–60 degrees to the ground when it contacts it. The power of the stroke comes from a firm pulling action with your right hand. Your head should be almost over the ball as you make the stroke.

By turning your right wrist, the head of the stick can be opened or closed so that the ball is pushed forwards or backwards to a team-mate. In midfield, you will find that the backward reverse push is extremely useful to keep possession and to change the direction of attack.

Reverse-stick hit

The reverse-stick hit is quite a difficult stroke, but is extremely useful — especially for players on the left side of the pitch. It is well worth persevering to develop this skill.

Grip and position
The grip is similar to the one you use for the forehand hit, but with the stick reversed so that the toe is pointing downwards. You will probably find the stroke easier if you slide your left hand a short distance down the handle. Most players hold the stick about 3–6 in (7.5–15 cm) from the top. Your right hand should be touching the left one.

Position yourself so that the ball is just in front of your right foot, with your body leaning forward so that your head is over the ball.

Technique
The hitting action is more of a firm tap than a full swing, so don't overdo the backswing. The power comes mainly from your wrists through a short snapping movement. Don't try to hit the ball too hard, or you will lose control of both your backswing and your balance.

AERIAL PASSES

Overhead passes are an important part of the modern game. They are an effective way of finding space behind opposing defenders into which your strikers can run. However, take care when you use an aerial stroke such as the flick or scoop — if you lift the ball in a way which will endanger players, you will be penalised.

The flick

The flick can be used to lift the ball into the air for long or short distances. This is important both in open play and at penalty strokes and penalty corners.

Grip and position
The grip and body position are similar to those used for the push, but for the flick the ball should be slightly ahead of the left foot.

Technique

Approach the ball with the stick sloping back towards you. Turn the face fully open with your right hand, and then push it forwards under the ball.

Transfer your body weight from your right leg to your left leg and "shovel" the ball into the air, powering it with your right arm. Keep your body down low until you feel the ball leave your stick. Your left hand controls the direction of the shot, as well as adding speed by pushing the top of the stick backwards with a whiplash action.

For scoops and flicks you must keep your body low until the ball has left the stick.

The reverse scoop

The reverse scoop is very useful for players on the left side of the pitch.

Grip

Twist the handle as if preparing for the reverse-stick push. Grip firmly with both hands.

Technique

The action is simple if you imagine that you are shovelling sand on a beach:

With your right foot forwards and the stick inclined back at about 45 degrees, lean over the ball and lift it into the air with a quick whipping action from your right hand. The power comes from your right hand: the left one should just guide and control the top of the stick. Experiment with the position of your right hand to see which gives you the greatest power.

7

Ball control

Receiving the ball, either from a team-mate or by intercepting an opponent's pass, calls for effective ball control. Developing what we term "strong" ball-control skills is an important part of becoming a good team player.

Receiving the ball

You do not necessarily have to stop the ball in order to receive it effectively; the object is to get it under control and into position for your next move in the shortest amount of time. Strong ball control means that, when you receive, you are able to keep your stick close to the ball and in the "push position" (see page 31), so that you can immediately look up for your next pass or prepare to avoid a tackle.

Receiving a ball coming straight to you
Hold your stick upright but inclined slightly forwards, so that the ball will stay on the ground after contact. Try to absorb the impact of the ball by relaxing the grip of your right hand until after impact.
　　Your footwork is very important — move into line with the ball as it approaches, and keep your body weight forward. Bend your knees, keep your head still and watch the ball right onto your stick.

Receiving the ball from your left
When the ball is coming from your left, allow it to come across in front of your body, and control it in front of your right foot. Cushion the ball onto the stick by relaxing the grip of your right hand. (See photograph on page 38.)

Receiving the ball from your right
Depending on the line of the pass, two different techniques can be used to receive a ball coming from your right:

A study in concentration as Andy Bailey receives a pass from his left.

Using the open stick

With the stick out to the right of your body, turn your shoulders to bring your head, eyes, hands and stick all in line with the ball as it approaches you. Then you can simply guide the ball quickly into a position ready for a forward run or a pass.

Using the reverse stick

This method will give you better vision to your left, and will allow you to move forward more quickly. As the ball comes from your right, let it pass across in front of your body and control it with the reverse stick when it is in front of your left foot, or just outside it.

Turn your stick with your left wrist and try to position your head directly above the ball with your body weight forward. Relax the grip of your right hand to "caress" the ball onto the stick head.

Receiving practices

Controlling the ball should be practised from a stationary position until you feel confident. Footwork, balance and watching the ball onto the stick are the keys to success. Once you feel confident, you can start to practise control on the move.

Concentrate! The way you first touch the ball when receiving a pass or intercepting determines how much time you have to make your next move. The difference between top internationals and good club players is often in the quality of their first touch. The top players anticipate the speed and direction of the ball accurately, and control the ball so quickly that their opponents can't dive in. The speed of control can be deceptive, however. Fast should not mean rushed: really good players often *seem* to have lots of time to make their next move.

Anticipation and speed of reaction are essential for gaining possession and keeping it.

8

Game skills

Beating your opponents

Vision

If you have possession of the ball and an opponent blocks your way down the field, you have to decide whether to try to dribble past the opposition or to pass to a team-mate. Whichever option you use, you will only succeed regularly if you develop good *vision*. Vision is the ability to see both the immediate area and the broader view. In the immediate area you judge your distance from an opponent and take in details such as the position of his feet; in the broader view you note the position of your team-mates — are they unmarked and ready to receive your pass? Where is the gap in the defence?

● Practise being able to scan the field while dribbling. Use your peripheral vision to help you keep control of the ball.

- Practise scanning the pitch just before you receive a pass, so that when you do get the ball you already know which passes are possible and what moves your team-mates are making.

The wall pass (one-two pass)

A pass is usually the best way to get past a challenge, and should be your first choice. The technique is to make a short pass to a team-mate, run past your opponent and then receive a return pass. This is called making a wall pass, because you are using your team-mate's stick to bounce the ball back to you, just as if you were bouncing it off a wall.

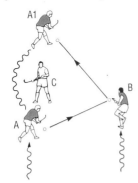

Figure 7 The wall pass: A makes a short pass to B, and then runs past his opponent C to A1, where he receives the return pass.

Dribbling past an opponent

You have to dribble around an opponent when you have no team-mates in support.

Beating an opponent on the open-stick side

This is the normal technique for beating someone approaching from your right:

- Approach at about two-thirds of your maximum speed, otherwise you may lose control.

- Veer towards your right, forcing the defender to transfer his weight to his left foot.

- Tap the ball to your left and accelerate past the defender.

- Once past, gather the ball and cut back to your right.

Figure 8 Beating an opponent on your open-stick side (see panel on page 32).

Beating an opponent on the reverse-stick side
This is almost a mirror-image of the previous example.

● Move the ball to your left to force your opponent's weight onto his right foot.

● Turn your stick into reverse position and drag the ball across to your right side as quickly as possible.

● Accelerate past, and then in behind your opponent.

Figure 9 Beating an opponent on the reverse-stick side is almost a mirror-image of the open-stick technique.

Beating an opponent by pushing the ball between his legs
This is a technique which you have to use quickly if the opportunity presents itself.

● Approach your opponent at a controlled speed.

● If there is space, gently push the ball between his feet, close to the left foot if possible.

● Accelerate past and collect the ball behind your opponent.

Figure 10 Pushing the ball between the opponent's feet

Deception
Apart from obvious alternative ways of beating an opponent, such as sheer speed or lifting the ball over the opponent's stick, you can also use deception. By looking in one direction and dodging in the other, you can throw an opponent off-balance. By dipping your right shoulder and dodging to your left, you can achieve the same effect. Practise these body and eye movements without the ball first, and see if you can fool a friend about which way you are going to run past him.

Shooting skills

Shooting at goal is a specialised skill which needs constant practice. Many teams have good defences and midfield play but fail to win games because of lack of composure in front of the goal. Always bear in mind the two basic principles of shooting:

1 Shoot early
If you possibly can, you should shoot for goal as soon as the ball enters the goal circle.

2 Follow-up
Another forward should always follow the ball after every shot, to try to pick up any rebounds off the goal-keeper's pads.

Quick backswing
Try to develop a short, quick backswing: gripping the stick slightly lower down will help with this. This shortened grip will speed up the backswing, which is vital for successful goal-scoring because defenders rarely give you time for a more leisurely shot.

Footwork
Practise shooting under all conditions. Repeat the shot until you can be accurate with your weight over either foot, or even when off-balance. The striker who can get a shot in regardless of the position of his body will be a most valuable team member.

Push shots and flick shots
Not all goal shots have to be hit; indeed, you won't always have time to lift your stick off the ball, so practise pushing and flicking the ball into the corners of the goal. Practise both open-stick and reverse-stick shooting in this way.

The player on the left has her stick reversed ready to take a shot at goal.

Rebounds

Many goals are scored from a follow-up shot after the goalkeeper has saved the initial shot. Practise by hitting or flicking a ball against a wall, collecting the rebound, and either slapping it straight back at the wall or controlling it before flicking it over an imaginary goal-keeper.

Goal awareness

Top-level forwards develop a goal sense or goal awareness so that they do not have to look up at goal before shooting. If you have practised hard at developing your peripheral vision, this will help you spot the goal-keeper's position.

Marking

Marking is the key to good defence and effective interception. Never let your opponents have room to operate freely: keep close to your opposite numbers so that their team-mates cannot safely pass to them.

You will often hear the expression "mark the player, not the ball". This is good advice to keep in mind. Good marking will deny the other team many opportunities to attack, and should increase your chances of making successful tackles.

Tight marking is a vital part of effective team play. However, you must always be aware of the fine line between tight marking and obstruction.

Tackling

Every member of a team must be able to tackle: winning possession of the ball must be a priority for any player whenever there is the opportunity. There are many components of good tackling:

General

- *Watch the ball* — not the stick or body of your opponent.

- *Close down your opponent's space* — quickly close the gap between you and your opponent to pressurise him.

- *Keep your balance* — don't dive in too fast and lose control.

- *Think footwork* — when you are close enough to tackle your opponent, stay in a side-on position with one foot in front of the other, rather like a boxer. Try to stay on your toes, with your weight on both feet, so that you can change direction quickly.

- *Timing your tackle* is vital because a lot of the time your opponent will have full control of the ball. Don't commit yourself too soon; use your footwork to make your opponent go to your right side if you can. Be ready to take advantage if the attacker loses control or lifts his stick off the ball.

This Scottish defender will have to time her tackle very precisely if she is to get the ball away from England's Jane Swinnerton without committing a stick tackle.

- *Use channelling* — you can force an opponent to try to go past you on your preferred side by leaving slightly more space on that side of your body. This will encourage the attacker to run that way, but you have the advantage of controlling where he is going. Good channelling allows your team-mates to cover you better and to make interceptions from the attacker's pass.

A straightforward challenge during a New Zealand v USA match

The open-side tackle

When tackling from the right, use this approach:

● Be well-balanced, with your left foot and shoulder leading. Hold the stick in your left hand.

● Take up a low position, with your knees bent and your eyes on the ball. Your stick should be close to the ground, and you must be ready to pounce as soon as your opponent takes his stick away from the ball.

● The tackle should be a sudden jab so that your stick makes a long flat barrier against the ball.

● Having made your tackle, get your right hand back on the stick so that you can control the ball as you move away.

The reverse-side tackle

Tackling from the left is much more difficult than from the right, so, whenever possible, you should try to channel the attacker onto your open-stick side. However, for players on the left side of the field this is often not possible, nor in the best interests of the team-mates who are covering them.

● When you tackle from the left, be level with your opponent, or just in front of him.

● Hold the stick in your left hand, but twist the grip so that the toe is pointing to the ground. You use the toe to trap the ball and drag it away from the attacker.

46

Competing for the ball. The player challenging from the left is making a good reverse-stick tackle.

● Your stick can be laid almost flat to provide a larger barrier, but you must be certain of winning the ball if you use this method, because if you miss the tackle, your opponent will be away before you can recover.

● Having made the tackle, get both hands back onto your stick and bring the ball quickly round to your strong right-side position.

● Remember the rule that when you tackle you must not touch the opponent's stick or body: it is very difficult to tackle an opponent from behind on the left side without breaking this rule.

The jab tackle

This tackle is made when your opponent is still in front of you. It is designed to surprise the attacker and catch him unawares.

● Hold your stick at the top with your left hand.

● Twist your wrist so that the back of the stick is facing the ground.

● As soon as you see the chance, jab the head of your stick "through" the ball: imagine that it is a boxer's jab or a snake's tongue.

Goalkeeping

Goalkeeping is a very exciting part of the game. If you want to be a goalkeeper you will need good concentration, courage, fast reactions and confidence. Your performance as a goalkeeper can win matches for your team, thrill spectators, and sometimes encourage your team-mates through a bad patch.

Saves are made with your kickers, leg-guards, hands and stick. No matter how keen you are, don't take up the position of goalkeeper if you do not have all the necessary protective equipment (see page 15).

Basic goalkeeping techniques

Stance
You must be balanced: whenever play is approaching your circle you must be ready to move or dive to either side.

● Your weight should be forward on the balls of your feet (heels off the ground).

● Bend your legs with your feet comfortably shoulder-width apart.

● Bend your back slightly so that your head is above your knees (the "chin-knee-toe" position).

● Hold your stick halfway down in your right hand, and have your left hand ready to stop any high shots.

Most of all, concentrate on keeping your *head forward*, as this will help to prevent you from falling over when making a save. A goalkeeper on the ground is hopeless because he has very little chance of saving any rebound shots.

Saves

The save–clear technique
Here the object is to save and clear a low ball in one movement, using a combination of body movement and the rebound qualities of your pads or kickers. Try to get your head over the line of the shot so that you can intercept it accurately, then turn your kicker to give the rebound angle you want. After saving the shot, bring your legs together to provide a larger barrier against any possible rebound shot.

Kicking to clear the ball
The goalie is the only player in the team who is allowed to kick the ball. If the shot does not rebound far enough away, you can kick the ball away with either instep to give clearance. This is not a very powerful way of kicking the ball, but it is quite accurate. However, if you can get the top of your foot to the ball, you will usually be able to kick the ball further.

For an effective kick, place your non-kicking foot beside the ball, and take a good swing with the kicking foot. If you keep your head over the ball and your body-weight forward, you will be able to keep the ball close to the ground.

Practise kicking with either leg, and try to avoid toe-punting (kicking with the toe of your boot). More often than not, toe punts result in a miskick.

A goalkeeper under pressure manages to get a foot to the ball and kick it away.

Saves with the hand or stick

You have the advantage of being the only player who can use his stick to stop the ball above shoulder-height — always provided that your action does not cause danger. Do remember that whatever you do, you are not allowed to catch the ball: a penalty stroke will be awarded against you if you do.

For high saves, keep your eye on the ball and try to get in line with it. Use your stick and left palm together to make a wide barrier. You can either deflect the ball around the goal or let it drop before kicking it clear.

Knowing the angles

Angles are vitally important to a goalkeeper. Practise in a full-sized goal and try to imagine a small "D" some 2 metres in radius from the centre of the goal. You are in the correct position when you stand on the edge of this "D" on a line between the centre of the goal and the line of the ball. You will quickly develop an understanding of when a shot is going wide, a skill vital to all goalkeepers.

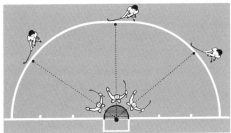

Figure 11

9

Fitness

You will enjoy your hockey much more if you keep fit. As with most field games, a hockey match calls for a lot of energy, and you will need all the four Ss:

● **Stamina** — so that you can keep running throughout the game or even a full tournament of games. During a 70-minute hockey game you will run between three and five miles (5–8 km).

● **Strength** — so that you can hit, push and shoot hard, as well as being able to win the ball with strong tackles.

● **Suppleness** — so that you can reach out to stop the ball or tackle at full stretch.

● **Speed** — so that you can reach the ball before the opponent who is marking you, and run away with it.

Stamina

You can develop your stamina by regular endurance training; distance running is the usual way of doing this. Start slowly, and gradually increase both your jogging speed and your distance until you are regularly doing runs of 2–5 miles (3–8 km). You should aim to run two or three times a week.

Another type of stamina training is *fartlek* running. This is a form of distance running which involves regular changes of pace: walk — jog — sprint full speed — walk — jog, and so on. Fartlek training can mirror the type of running you need to do in a game. If a group of you do this training together, it can be great fun. Regular repetition is the key to success, so try to cover at least two miles (3 km) three times a week.

Some players concentrate on repetition runs on an athletics track to build stamina. This form of training consists of a series of long sprints and runs over distances up to 800 m (880 yd). After each sprint or run, you rest for a time equal to the duration of that run. A

Hockey is a fast running-and-chasing game: overall fitness can make all the difference, especially in the second half of a match.

simple programme to start with would be: run 800 m, rest for two minutes; run 400 m (440 yd) twice, resting for one minute after each 400; run 200 m (220 yd) three times, resting for 30 seconds after each 200.

Strength

Weight-training and young people
Strength is of benefit to any sport player, but young people who are still growing should not take part in weight-training or significant overload-training as this may affect bone development and cause joint damage.

If you are tempted to use weights or a multi-gym in a sports centre, it is most important to take advice from an experienced trainer, coach or teacher. By using exercises which use your own body weight to apply loads, you can build up basic strength without multi-gyms or weights.

Sit-ups
Sit on the floor or an inclined bench with your feet flat, knees bent and hands alongside your ears. Pull yourself up until your elbows touch your knees, and then gently lower yourself down until your elbows are flat on the floor (or bench). Repeat as many times as you can.

Make sure your knees are bent: there is a risk of straining your lower back if you try sit-ups with straight legs.

Press-ups
Take up the front-support position (see diagram), keeping your back straight. Lower yourself until your nose and chest touch the floor, and then push up to straighten your arms again. Repeat...

Squat jumps
Squat with your knees bent and fingers touching the floor, then jump up as high as you can, throwing your arms upwards at the same time. Repeat as many times as possible.

Wrist rolls
Strong wrists and forearms will help you to hit the ball hard, tackle strongly, and push or flick the ball over long distances. You can develop wrist strength simply by squeezing a small rubber ball — a squash ball is just the right size — whenever you can. However, *wrist rolls* are a favourite with hockey players, and give good results.

Tie a brick or similar weight to a piece of cord about five feet (1.5 m) long, and tie the other end to the centre of your stick. Holding your hands out in front of you, roll the stick so the the weight is lifted to it; then unroll the cord so that the weight is lowered to the ground again, keeping control throughout its descent. Repeat as many times as you can.

Suppleness

All sportspeople need to develop good flexibility. Being supple reduces the risk of damaging muscles and ligaments during a game or practice session.

You should limber up and stretch before every training session or match, but try to get into the habit of warming up and stretching every day. My simple routine starts at the top of your body and works downwards:

Neck

● Drop your head forward and slowly rotate it in a wide circle, five times one way and then five the other.

Arms, shoulders and chest

● *Full-arm circling*: Stand with your back straight and make large circles with your arms, keeping them straight throughout, and brushing your ears and thighs on each rotation. Circle five times forwards and five times backwards.

- *Elbow pulls*: With your arms bent overhead, grasp one elbow with your opposite hand and gently pull your elbow behind your head. Repeat three times for each arm.

Back and spine

- *Rotation*: Lie flat with your arms out in a "T" position. Lift your right leg and try to touch your left hand with your right foot while keeping your shoulder-blades on the floor. Repeat three times for each leg.

- *Sideways flexion*: Stand upright. Slide your right arm down the side of your right leg as far as you can without leaning forwards. Repeat three times for each leg.

- *Back extension*: Starting in the press-up (front-support) position, arch your back by pushing your hips onto the ground and looking up at the sky. Hold the position for five seconds, then turn over and roll up into a ball. Repeat three times.

Hips

● Lie flat on your back with one leg straight. Grasp your other knee with both hands and pull it tight to your chest. Repeat three times for each leg.

Groin

● Sit with your legs as wide apart as possible and bend forward from the hips *without bending your knees*. Reach out with your hands as far as possible in front of you, and then down each leg in turn.

Quadriceps

● Stand on one leg and pull your other ankle up against your bottom. Repeat three times for each leg.

Hamstrings

● Bend forward and trap your fingers under your toes. Then slowly try to straighten your legs. Repeat three times, holding the stretch for five seconds each time.

Calves

● Stand with both feet pointing the same way, and step forward with one leg. Keep both feet flat on the ground and gently push your hips forwards and downwards. Repeat three times for each leg.

Strength alone is not enough: good balance gives you the ability to dodge and sprint to get the ball or to keep it.

Speed

Possession wins games, and if you can sprint quickly, you will always have the best chance of beating your opponents to the ball. You can develop speed, but only if you have first developed good stamina, strength and suppleness. Try some of these exercises two to three times a week:

Shuttle run

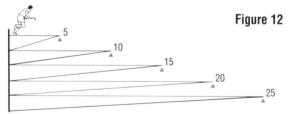

Figure 12

Set markers at 5, 10, 15, 20 and 25 yards (or metres) from a line. Run to the first marker, then back to the start line, run to the second marker, then back to the start line, and so on. Running continuously, this shuttle should take you between 28 and 35 seconds. Rest for 30 seconds and repeat. Do this six times. Shuttle running is very tiring, but excellent for developing speed over short distances, and the speed on the turn which is so vital in hockey.

You can make shuttle running more realistic by doing it while holding your stick: run out to the markers with the head of the stick on the ground all the way, and then turn and sprint back holding it in one hand.

Zig-zag sprint

Hockey is a mixture of straight sprints, turns to left and right, and abrupt stops. To simulate this, try the zig-zag sprint:

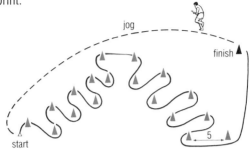

Figure 13 Place the markers about 5 metres apart.

Sprint round the course as shown in Figure 13, then jog back to the start. Rest two minutes between each run. You should try to build up to five laps dribbling the ball around the markers, followed by five laps sprinting while holding your stick in your right hand.

Continuous relay

This form of training is good fun for all the team.

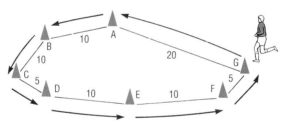

Figure 14 Continuous relay; the distances shown are examples only.

When setting out the markers in the circle, ensure that the distances between them are varied.

A player stands at each marker. When the whistle is blown, *A* sprints and tags *B* who then rushes to *C*, and so on. *G* has to sprint round to tag *A*, who again sets off to start the next lap. The exercise is continued until everyone has had enough! Try for at least six laps of the circle.

10

Improving your game

Like any other sport, you won't improve in hockey if you don't practise. You should try to practise your individual ball skills as often as possible. You can do a lot of practising on your own, although it can be more fun if you can get a group together.

For most of these practices you will need some markers or targets; these need not be special — you can use cones, bricks, plastic bottles or bags of sand. Run the courses in both directions, and always try to improve your times.

Dribbling practices

Open-side dribble
Place markers ten yards (or metres) apart and dribble the ball along the path shown in Figure 15 using your open stick only.

Figure 15

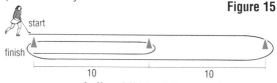

Indian dribble slalom
Lay out a circuit of several markers, and dribble the ball around them using the reverse stick to move the ball from left to right round every other marker. Concentrate on ball control.

Figure 16

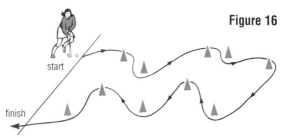

The stop dribble

Dribble to one marker, then stop the ball dead, change direction and dribble to the next marker. If you are practising on an area such as a tennis court or pavement which has lines marked on it, you can use the lines instead of markers.

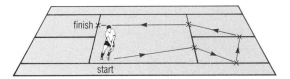

Figure 17 The stop dribble. Stop the ball dead at the markers, or — as here — when the ball crosses one of the lines.

Passing practices

Practise the push, hit and flick strokes by making a circuit of markers to dribble through before pushing, hitting or flicking the ball at a target.

Concentrate on bringing the ball quickly into the correct position, then work on the power and accuracy of the shot.

A variation is to line up several balls and shoot them at the target as rapidly as possible. Score your shots and try to beat your friends.

Receiving practices

The best way to practise receiving skills is with a partner, but don't worry if no one else is available: you can use a wall to bounce your own pass back. Practise to your open and reverse sides. Variety can be introduced by using a tennis ball to change the speed of the returns, and by using hits, flicks and pushes to hit the ball against the wall.

Shooting practices

Top goalscorers have the ability to shoot from all angles, no matter where the ball may arrive in relation to their feet. You can practise this on your own, bouncing passes off a wall before shooting at a target. Use pushes and flicks as well as hits, and make it difficult for yourself by shooting with either foot forward and at different distances from your body. Concentrate on speed, and change your position relative to the wall, so that passes come from both right and left.

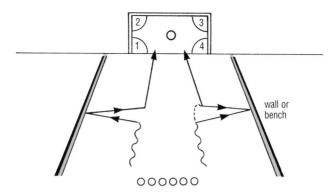

Figure 18 Good shooting practice can be had on your own by bouncing the ball off a wall or bench (to simulate a pass from a team-mate) and then shooting at a target — perhaps one particular area of the goal.

You can further complicate your task by setting out marker cones as if they were defenders, and trying to avoid them.

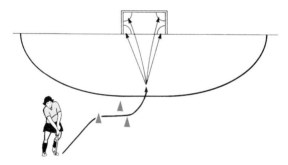

Figure 19 On the hockey pitch, you can practise beating the defenders as well as shooting. Unfortunately real opponents are not so easy to beat as marker cones!

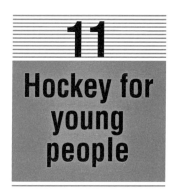

11

Hockey for young people

Youngsters who try to play the full eleven-a-side game too soon tend to become isolated from the action and may lose interest. To overcome this problem, mini-hockey and colts hockey have been developed. These games are the hockey equivalent of five-a-side football, and most youngsters find them more exciting to play than the full adult game.

Both games are played on a small area — usually across the width of a full-size pitch. This gives young players the fun and excitement of always being involved, no matter where the ball is on the pitch.

Mini-hockey and colts hockey are played by two teams of not more than seven players each, and there are fewer rules than in the full game, so that play flows more readily.

Mini-hockey

Mini-hockey is played with a relatively soft, light ball. A match normally comprises two halves of ten minutes each way.

Mini-hockey: the perfect introduction to the game

The main differences from adult hockey are:

- There are no shooting circles.
- Goals can be scored from anywhere on the pitch.
- There is no offside rule.
- After fouls or infringements, the game is restarted by a free hit or push. These re-starts are not held within ten yards (9.14 m) of a goal.

Mini-hockey is an excellent introduction to the game for players up to about 12 years of age.

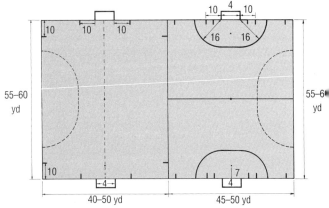

Figure 20 The full-size hockey pitch can be divided in half, with one half (the left side in the diagram) being used for mini-hockey and the other half for colts hockey. The goals and shooting circles are full-size, but the field of play is considerably smaller, making the game much easier for young players.

Colts hockey

Colts hockey is a stage nearer to the full game. It is aimed at players aged between 12 and 18. Up to the age of about 14, mixed games are appropriate because there is little difference in strength between boys and girls.

A match normally comprises two halves of 15 minutes each way.

Colts hockey introduces the scoring circle, the penalty corner and the offside rule, just as in the full-sized game. However, the small pitch ensures that everybody shares in the action.

For both mini-hockey and colts hockey, it is best to have two or three substitutes per team, and for substitutions to take place at any time to make sure that everyone takes part.

Getting started

Hockey is still played in many girls' schools, and this is still the most usual way to get into the game. In most countries it is far less common for boys to enter the game through the school system.

Even if you have had the good fortune to play at school, you will probably need to join a club to continue your hockey career.

Your school PE teacher will almost certainly have details of local clubs. Progressive clubs offer regular coaching to new players, and send circulars around the local schools encouraging newcomers to join. Your PE teacher will also have received details of coaching courses available to you.

There will be probably be two or three clubs in your area. Don't join the first one you find! Do some research. There are good clubs and not-so-good clubs. Before you join, make sure the club offers regular coaching sessions and has a good youth policy. Modern, go-ahead clubs run colts and mini-hockey festivals and tournaments. Choose your club carefully; it may well determine the speed at which you develop as a skilful player.

In Britain, if your school really cannot help, there are plenty of other ways of finding a club: phone the recreation department of your local authority, or enquire at a public library. Your local Sports Council office will have information, or you can contact your governing body of hockey (see addresses on page 64).

Instruction at school continues to play a vital part in the development of hockey.

Useful addresses

Great Britain

The Hockey Association
16 Northdown Street
London
N1 9BG

The Irish Hockey Union
7 Barnhill Avenue
Dalkey
Co Dublin

The Scottish Hockey Union
Caledonia House
South Gyle
Edinburgh
EH12 9DQ

The Welsh Hockey Association
1 White Hart Lane
Caerleon
Monmouthshire
NP6 1AB

Overseas

The Australian Hockey
   Association
Suite 1
36 Park Street
South Melbourne 3205
Australia

The Canadian Field Hockey
   Association
1600 James Naismith Drive
Gloucester
Ontario
K1B 5N4
Canada

The New Zealand Hockey
   Federation
PO Box 24024
Royal Oak
Auckland
New Zealand

The Field Hockey Association of
   America
1750 East Boulder Street
Colorado Springs
Colorado 80909
USA

International

Fédération Internationale de Hockey
Avenue des Arts 1
PO Box 5
1040 Brussels
Belgium